Original title:
Golden Pollen Poetry

Copyright © 2025 Creative Arts Management OÜ
All rights reserved.

Author: Juliana Wentworth
ISBN HARDBACK: 978-1-80566-782-7
ISBN PAPERBACK: 978-1-80566-802-2

Dappled Light Upon The Earth

Sunlight dances with glee,
Tickling leaves on the tree.
Bees buzz with a silly song,
Nature's party won't last long!

Tides of Blooming Splendor

Flowers march in a parade,
Each petal a colorful trade.
They sway with laughter and cheer,
Giving the wind a good ear.

Beneath the Glare of Midday

Squirrels crack jokes in the shade,
While sunflowers wear their upgrade.
A frog croaks like a rock star,
As clouds gather... oh, how bizarre!

The Language of Blooming

Daisies wink with a bright eye,
Tulips set off fireworks in the sky.
The garden buzzes with chatter,
While ants compete on who's the better platter.

The Gentle Kiss of the Harvest

In fields where cornflakes gleam so bright,
The scarecrow dances, quite a sight!
He winks at beans, with swagger, oh!
While squirrels plot their nutty show.

The pumpkins giggle, round and fat,
They wear fine hats—a cozy spat!
They roll and bounce in playful cheer,
Laughing at crows that can't get near.

The sun, it tickles every sprout,
While bees joke loudly, buzzing about!
A honey-dripping pun is spun,
As flowers blush beneath the sun.

Oh, harvest time, you crafty muse,
With carrots dressed in tiny shoes!
They hop along to share a feast,
With laughter loud, we're never least.

Essence of Radiant Moments

In fields where laughter roams,
Buzz of bees makes their homes,
Jigging flowers with glee,
Dancing on a bumblebee.

Petals dressed in sunshine,
Wobble on a vine, divine,
Sipping nectar so sweet,
Bees tap dance to the beat.

Grasshoppers join in spree,
With frogs croaking a decree,
Laughter echoes through the air,
As blossoms sway without a care.

Sunbeam tickles the leaves,
Whispers secrets, then deceives,
A butterfly in a whirl,
Painting smiles with each twirl.

Crescendo of the Bloom

Petals burst like confetti,
Pollen floats, feeling heady,
Dolls of daisies, we cheer,
With a giggle, spring is here.

Bees recite their busy verse,
Pollination, not a curse,
Fluttering with silly pride,
As daisies wink, side by side.

Chasing shadows, what a show,
Wobbly blooms all in a row,
Sunny days and silly fights,
Nature's stage hosts wild delights.

Bouncing beans on a spree,
Swaying softly by the tree,
Frogs croak out a giggly tune,
As flowers laugh beneath the moon.

A Glimpse of Gilded Frolic

Flowers donned in frolic wear,
Jumping jacks in breezy air,
Bumblebees in a race,
Buzzing with a happy face.

Ladybugs in polka dots,
Join the party, thanks a lot,
A petal's song, oh what a sight,
With every twirl, they take flight.

Ants parade on tiny feet,
Joining in with sprightly beat,
The daisies prance, oh what fun,
Chasing shadows 'til they're done.

Sprightly blooms with jokes to share,
Whirlwinds of color everywhere,
Even the sun can't resist,
As laughter leaves a golden mist.

Sweet Alchemy Underfoot

In gardens where the laughter grows,
Silly sprouts in endless rows,
With winks and giggles, they bloom,
Creating laughter that fills the room.

Frolicking through petals' delight,
While squirrels plan a daring flight,
Beneath the blooms, secrets lie,
As butterflies twirl and fly high.

Dandelions puff out their seeds,
Sprinkling wishes, growing weeds,
Each plucky breeze brings a chuckle,
As the flowers share their cuddle.

With every step, a dance unfolds,
Beneath the sun, a tale retolds,
Nature's fun in vibrant hue,
Oh, what wonders she can do!

Blossoms in Liquid Gold

The flowers giggle in the breeze,
They're wearing sunshine with such ease.
A bee slips on a bright tuxedo,
Dancing 'round like he's a weirdo.

Petals whisper, 'What a show!'
Their colors rival every glow.
Oh, watch the clumsy bugs that trip,
In this nectar-sipping circus trip!

Threads of Sunlight Weaved

Sunlight's fibers, soft and warm,
Weave through petals, a quaint charm.
The dandelion's puffed up head,
Sends fluffy wishes, dreams widespread.

Butterflies in fancy suits,
Flit about with jolly roots.
They sip their drinks and laugh away,
Like they're at a garden play!

Rapture Amongst Blossoms

In a riot of colors so bright,
Blossoms buzz with pure delight.
A ladybug slips on a leaf,
While ants parade, causing grief.

With petals painted like a laugh,
Nature sketches a silly path.
Crickets chirp a tune so sweet,
That even flowers move their feet!

Fragrance of Dawn's Promise

Morning opens with a grin,
While flowers break into a spin.
The jasmine jokes with the sweet rose,
And morning glories strike a pose.

A hummingbird zooms to say hi,
While clouds above toss candy spry.
With laughter tickling the air,
Nature dances without a care!

Carpeting the Ground in Light

A carpet made of sunny cheer,
Each step feels like springtime here.
The ants all dance, they shimmy and sway,
In this light-hearted, pollen play.

The daisies giggle in vibrant hues,
While bees wear tuxedos, sipping on dues.
A parade of colors, a jolly sight,
Under the magic of morning light.

Golden Threads of Earth

Threads of laughter weave through air,
As flowers gossip without a care.
The sun tickles petals, a joyful tease,
While plants share stories with the breeze.

Dandelions wish on whims of flies,
Spreading their dreams beneath bright skies.
In this tapestry, smiles are found,
Each stitch a chuckle sewn in the ground.

A Symphony of Dust and Sun

A symphony plays with dust and light,
Where giggling blooms take off in flight.
The pollen floats like tiny boats,
Sailing on whispers and sunny notes.

Grasshoppers hum their tunes so fine,
While ladybugs waltz, their colors align.
In this orchard of laughter and glee,
Nature's orchestra conducts with glee.

The Delicate Touch of Flora

With a delicate touch, the flowers conspire,
To tickle the toes of a bumbling choir.
They sway with joy, in a breezy dance,
As bunnies hop in a merry trance.

Petals prank the unsuspecting bees,
Who stumble about, in sheer unease.
In this garden of whimsy and play,
Flora's charm brightens the day.

The Sunlit Tapestry

In the meadow, sunbeams play,
Dancing flowers in array,
Buzzing bees, a wobbly sight,
Sip their way through morning light.

Frogs in hats and dancing shoes,
Join the fun, they have the blues,
Their croaks are tunes, a ribbit cheer,
This sunny scene, oh, don't be near!

Luminous Images of Spring

Hopping rabbits, oh so spry,
In a springtime pie up high,
Chasing shadows, what a race,
Bouncing round with silly grace.

Clouds are giggling, skies so bright,
Painting rainbows, pure delight,
Squirrels juggling acorns high,
Underneath the laughing sky.

Nectar's Gentle Allure

Buzzing whispers fill the air,
Flowers wear their best debonair,
With nectar sweet and scents divine,
Bees throw parties, oh, how they dine!

Moths in bow ties swoon and prance,
Fluttering in a crafty dance,
The hummingbird's a speedy guest,
In this banquet, they're the best!

Garden of Infinite Whispers

In a garden where jokes sprout,
Every flower sees a route,
Petals giggle, gossip flows,
Wind tells tales that no one knows.

Gnomes with glasses, wise and bold,
Share a riddle, bright and old,
Whimsical whispers, chuckles blend,
In this garden, joy won't end.

Ambrosial Dreams

In fields where bumblebees dance bold,
Honey flows like the tales we've told.
Chasing butterflies in silly hats,
Laughing at squirrels, we've made such chitchats.

Sweet nectar drips from rosy plumes,
While dreaming of jam in fruit-filled rooms.
A picnic planned with no real food,
Just jellied giggles and honeyed mood.

Stardust from Blossoms

Petals shimmer like disco balls,
As bees break out in buzzing brawls.
In gardens where imagination thrives,
Fairies prank cats and ancient hives.

Moonlight tickles the daisy's face,
While critters gather for a wild race.
Laughter echoing through flower beds,
Worms wear glasses to show fancy threads.

Hushed Secrets of the Grove

In the grove, a secret meeting waits,
Where frogs play chess and gossip states.
Birds in ties discuss the best tunes,
While raccoons debate under silver moons.

Sneaky squirrels tell tales with flair,
Trading nuts for wisdom and some rare air.
In whispers, petals unfold their schemes,
As trees recite outlandish dreams.

The Blooming Chorus

A chorus springs from blossoms bright,
With daisies singing under starlit night.
Bumblebees buzz a catchy refrain,
While butterflies twirl in a sweet campaign.

Every sprout has a solo to share,
With ladybugs clapping in the warm air.
Laughter blooms in the sunlight's gleam,
As nature joins in a whimsical dream.

Echoing Sunshine

In a garden where bees laugh,
They buzz like they're on a path.
Flowers giggle in bright hues,
As I chase them in my shoes.

A butterfly plays tag with friends,
A game that never truly ends.
Sunshine tickles the petals' face,
In this wild and silly place.

The Poetics of Pollination

A bee with style, wearing shades,
Dances through the flowery parades.
Each flower winks with glee and cheer,
As buzzers promote the floral sphere.

Daffodils are stand-up comics bold,
With punchlines wrapped in bright and gold.
I laugh until my sides are sore,
This garden's joy is never a bore.

Beneath the Canopy of Dreams

Under leaves where dandelions spin,
Squirrels giggle at my silly grin.
Their chatter blends with a warm breeze,
As I trip over my own two knees.

In the shade where laughter blooms,
The air is filled with funny tunes.
Pollinating jokes take flight,
While I dance jumbled in delight.

Serenading the Burst of Color

Bees composing a joyful song,
Flutter here and there, all day long.
Colors clash in a playful shout,
As butterflies swirl, no doubt about.

Petals prance in a light ballet,
As I marvel at their cheeky display.
Nature's paintbrush runs wild and free,
Tickling every eyesore, you see!

Honeyed Harmony

In a garden where bees all buzz,
Petals tremble with joyful fuzz.
A chicken dons a floral cap,
Clucking tunes in a happy clap.

Butterflies waltz in the sun,
Thinking of nectar—oh, what fun!
A snail slides by in a tuxedo,
Who knew a garden could steal the show?

Bees do the tango, such a sight,
While ants march home without a fright.
The flowers giggle, petals sway,
As nature dances the day away.

So if you seek a laugh or two,
Step into this world—it's waiting for you!
With honeyed harmony all around,
Where joy and laughter are easily found.

The Call of Early Morn

When roosters croon their dawn duet,
The sleepy world can't quite forget.
A squirrel spills his nutty stash,
As sleepyheads shout, 'Oh, what a crash!'

Sunbeams poke through leafy trees,
Awaking all with playful ease.
A cat yawns wide, eyeing the show,
While waking leaves whisper low and slow.

The day is fresh, a blank canvas,
Filled with giggles and a bit of madness.
So rise and shine, embrace the glee,
In this morning's whimsical spree!

With breakfast toast and coffee cheer,
We stomp on ants, without a fear.
The call of early morn's a blast,
We laugh and play—it never lasts!

Dawn's Dappled Brush

Dawn dips its brush in colors new,
Painting skies a lovely hue.
A clownfish jokes with a sleeping cat,
'Is it morning already? Imagine that!'

Clouds fluff pillows in the sky,
As February penguins stroll by.
A raccoon in a beret strides,
Holding a croissant while he glides.

The sun starts to tickle the flowers' heads,
While sleepy bugs peek from their beds.
A jumpy frog sings a silly tune,
It's a morning party—our own cartoon!

So with a wink, we catch the light,
Dancing along with sheer delight.
Dawn's dappled brush makes us grin wide,
In this splendid, radiant ride.

Petals on a Gentle Gale

Petals swirl in the breeze that speaks,
Tickling noses, playing tricks.
A puppy chases the fluttering fun,
Wobbling awkwardly under the sun.

Dandelion wishes fly with glee,
The wind hums a tune, deliciously free.
A pig in overalls takes a turn,
Spinning dreams with every churn.

Butterflies giggle, they take to flight,
While daisies turn red from sheer delight.
Each petal whispers a silly pun,
As laughter rolls out—oh, what a run!

So join the frolic and don't be shy,
Let whimsies dance and laughter fly.
With petals on a gentle gale,
We'll paint the day with joy—no fail!

Dances in the Breeze

Butterflies throw a party, skies are blue,
They spin and twirl, like they've got a cue.
Flowers bounce to the rhythm in fright,
Bees join the dance, buzzing with delight.

A ladybug winks, dressed in red,
Tells the daisies, "Just follow my spread!"
The wind starts chuckling, laughing with grace,
As clovers groove, each finds their place.

The Pulse of Nature's Sigh

The trees shake their leaves, cracking a grin,
Whispering secrets, where has it been?
A fox in a tux, offers a jest,
Says nature's pulse beats on, well-dressed!

The river giggles, bubbling with cheer,
Tickling the rocks, "I'm crystal clear!"
Sunlight plays tag, darting through space,
And shadows take turns, licking their face.

Sunlight Draped in Petals

Sunlight lounges on a lily's face,
"Don't disturb me—I'm in my warm place!"
A sunflower yawns, stretching out wide,
As daisies all giggle, feeling spry inside.

Petals hold secrets, from whispers of rain,
Winking at clouds, "Come dance in my lane!"
Each drop a punchline, a laugh from afar,
Nature's own comedians, starring each star.

Colors Singing from the Soil

Worms in the dirt hum a jolly tune,
Painting the ground beneath the full moon.
The onions giggle, "Here comes the flood!"
While carrots chuckle, all muddy and stud.

Colors burst forth, in a riotous feud,
With reds and blues having a food mood.
A rainbow bows, takes a bow with a grin,
Says, "Let's all get messy, come join in on the din!"

Fields of Radiance

In fields where colors play,
Bees buzz with joy all day.
Flowers prance in bright array,
Chasing each cloud that goes astray.

Laughter spills from petals wide,
As they dance with pollen's guide.
Bumblebees in sneakers glide,
On a flowery joyride!

Glistening Petals Under Moonlight

In moonlight's silver glow,
Petals shine, a funny show.
Crickets chirp a dance routine,
While flowers tease with hues unseen.

A snail slips in a disco spin,
Winks at blooms and jumps right in.
Fireflies flicker, a twinkling grin,
Nature's party, let's begin!

The Alchemy of Bloom

Turning sunlight into cheer,
Each blossom feels so dear.
With giggles caught in every hue,
They mix up laughter like it's stew!

A dandelion can't contain,
Its wishes swirling in the rain.
Petal potion, quite the gain,
Turns old grass into a lane!

Sun-Kissed Fragments

A sunbeam slides on leafy greens,
Tickles petals, makes them preen.
Roses blush in vibrant schemes,
While daisies plot their frothy dreams.

Joking bees bring sticky news,
Wearing pollen like great shoes.
They dance in circles, hum and cruise,
In a game no one can lose!

Harvested Dreams

In the field of whimsical fate,
Dreams are plucked, not a moment too late.
They wiggle and jiggle, so hard to catch,
Like slippery fish, they're quite the match.

Baskets overflow, with thoughts that sway,
Some are hopeful, while others just play.
A sprinkle of laughter, a hint of jest,
Who knew that harvesting dreams could be best!

Stardust Sprinkled Beneath the Boughs

Under boughs where giggles bloom,
I trip on roots, but that's just my zoom.
Stardust glitters, a magical sight,
I blame my missteps on the starry night.

Ladybugs dance with a rhythm so sweet,
Buzzing around, they march on tiny feet.
Whispers of joy rise up in the air,
As I tumble and giggle, without a care!

Glimmers of Life

Life's little glimmers wink and shine,
Like fireflies caught in a glass of wine.
Chasing their flicker, I trip on a shoe,
But can't help but laugh, 'cause life's just a zoo.

With every misstep, a giggle comes forth,
Laughter spreads wide, it's truly of worth.
Glimmers twinkle, they spark and they play,
Turning fumbles to gifts in the silliest way!

Elysian Fields in Span

In fields of joy, I skip and hop,
With daisies tickling my toes, I drop.
The breeze blows gently, a playful tease,
As I pretend to dance with the bees.

Clouds above shape creatures that grin,
A dragon that giggles, a bear with a spin.
Under the sun, absurdly grand,
I trip through Elysium, feeling so planned!

Light's Embrace on Fragile Wings

Tiny bugs dance in the sun,
Wings like glitter, oh what fun!
They sip the nectar, oh so sweet,
While dodging feet on summer's street.

They flirt with flowers, oh so bold,
Whispering secrets, stories told.
With every flap, they seem to laugh,
A buzzing joy, like nature's craft.

In the meadow, where colors play,
A silly breeze carries dreams away.
With every gust, they twirl and spin,
These tiny dancers, full of grin.

As shadows grow and daylight fades,
They play hide and seek in sunny glades.
With every flutter, laughter rings,
In nature's circus, joy takes wing.

Nature's Whispered Elegy

Leaves chuckle softly in the breeze,
Tickling branches like silly tease.
The river giggles as it flows,
With splashy glee, it steals the show.

Squirrels plan a nutty heist,
Hiding treasures, oh, what a feast!
With twitching tails, they plot their fun,
While birds watch on, their beaks come undone.

A tree stump sits with a stoic grin,
As fungi rise, let the games begin!
They play hopscotch, sproutling sprout,
In nature's playground, there's no doubt.

But as dusk falls, the giggles wane,
Nature winks, not one bit vain.
In whispered tones, her tales unfold,
In solemn rapture, warmth and gold.

Summer's Sweet Caress

Oh summer, you tease with your warm embrace,
Splashing kids in the sunlit space.
Frogs croak jokes in the lily pond,
While blossoms yawn and grow quite fond.

Bumblebees buzz with a hint of sass,
Chasing shadows as they pass.
With each petal, a giggle is shared,
In this riotous garden, naught is spared.

Clouds form castles in the azure sky,
While ice cream drips, oh my, oh my!
A sunburned nose from too much play,
Nature's jest in a summer ballet.

As twilight falls with a wink and grin,
Fireflies twinkle, let the night begin.
In this season of laughter, life ignites,
With joy wrapped tightly in moonbeam lights.

The Luminous Harvest

Fields of corn dance in the breeze,
Joking with crows, a nature tease.
Pumpkins giggle, dressed in green,
While hay bales play, a sight serene.

The farmers chuckle, tales they weave,
Of crops so grand, they almost believe!
With buckets full of laughter stored,
They harvest joy from their rich hoard.

The apples blush in the orchard's light,
Playing hide and seek, a pure delight.
While critters chatter, crafting schemes,
In this glowing garden of whimsical dreams.

As moonlight spills on fields aglow,
Nature laughs, putting on a show.
The luminous harvest, a comedy bright,
Where joy and laughter take their flight.

soft touches of sunlight

The sunlight dances on my nose,
Like a dog that knows it's time to doze.
I squint and grin, what a sight!
Is it morning or just a dandelion's light?

A hat made of shade, I wear with flair,
My sunblock smeared everywhere!
The bees buzz by as if to say,
"Why don't you join us, hip-hip-hooray?"

Forget my coffee, I'll take this gleam,
I've found my joy in a sunlit dream.
Sun-kissed mischief, oh what a tease,
I'll dance like a leaf on a summer's breeze.

the artistry of decay

The leaves drop down, they twist and twirl,
   Nature's confetti in a graceful swirl.
  Each crunchy step is a work of art,
   A masterpiece made to break my heart.

  Old fences creak, they tell a joke,
   Whispering secrets in a dusty cloak.
What's that? A raccoon with a little flair—
Dressed in the remnants of yesterday's fair!

  The beauty of rust, oh how it glints,
Like a pair of shoes that won't give hints.
 Decay might smell, but let's not forget,
   It's a comedic play we can all regret!

echoes of the spring bloom

When blooms arrive, I jump with glee,
But so do the bunnies—what's wrong with me?
I plant my seeds in rows so neat,
Only to find they've turned into a buffet treat!

The tulips tease, they shake and sway,
"Pick us, pluck us, we'll brighten your day."
But pointy thorns are what I reap,
A florist's nightmare when I can't keep.

Squirrels take cover, I'm losing my mind,
Chasing birds, I'm far behind.
Yet with every sneeze, and all that's in bloom,
I find laughter amidst the perfume.

vein of the earth's vibrancy

In the soil's embrace, I dip my toes,
Unruly worms put on a show,
"Is that a grape?" I squint and stare—
Just a big lump of earthy flair!

The roots gossip beneath my feet,
"Don't you dare disturb our beat!"
I giggle at flowers, prancing about,
"Who needs a dancer? We've got sprout clout!"

With each heartbeat of the grassy lane,
How can I resist this joyful strain?
Nature's humor, it brightens my day,
In the vein of the earth, I laugh and sway.

humming of nature's symphony

A frog croaks loud, a merry tune,
Bees are buzzing, all afternoon.
The grasshoppers dance, in a silly way,
Mocking the wind, as it sways away.

Birds chirp jokes, in a feathery crew,
While ants scout food, in a line so true.
The sun winks bright, with a goofy grin,
Nature's concert, let the fun begin!

Trees sway and twist, in humorous arcs,
While squirrels play chess with acorn sparks.
A beetle rolls on, his prize so grand,
In the great outdoors, where laughter's planned.

Frolicsome whispers weave through the air,
In this wild show, there's no time to spare.
Nature's symphony, what a silly scene,
A laugh out loud, in vibrant green!

whispers of sweet surrender

A dandelion floats, with dreams so light,
A breeze tickles petals, a comical sight.
Bees take a tumble, then buzz with a cheer,
While flowers giggle, "Come join us here!"

The sun peeks over, in a sleepy stretch,
As ladybugs plan a tea party sketch.
With tiny cups made of dew and delight,
They toast to the sky, 'What a glorious night!'

Trees sway with laughter, branches collide,
In the dance of surrender, there's nothing to hide.
Their leaves share secrets in the soft glow,
Of a world that just laughs, with nowhere to go.

Whispers drift softly, with a wink and a tease,
In a playful embrace, the heart finds its ease.
Nature's comedy show puts on quite a splendor,
In the theater of life, we joyously wander.

dreams sewn in bright arrays

In the garden of giggles, dreams take flight,
A patch of bright flowers, a wonderful sight.
With petals like smiles, they bounce and they sway,
Sewing up laughter, in a jolly display.

Butterflies waltz with a whimsical twist,
While bugs tap dance, you get the gist.
Each bloom has a story, a tale of delight,
In colors so vivid, they brighten the night.

A squirrel does stand-up, with jokes oh-so-clear,
While hedgehogs chuckle, they've nothing to fear.
Up above, clouds drift like cotton candy fluffs,
In this world of dreams, we can't get enough!

Wonders are stitched in bright, playful threads,
As laughter bursts forth, from all the flower beds.
In this garden of joy, where each moment stays,
We revel in life's sweet, sunlit displays.

reflections of vibrant grace

In puddles of joy, the world finds its face,
A mirror of laughter, in nature's embrace.
Each ripple a chuckle, a giggle anew,
Where shadows of flora dance, silly yet true.

A cat in a sunbeam, stretched out in flair,
While butterflies tease, as they float in the air.
In this vibrant chaos, all creatures partake,
Finding grace in their blunders, make no mistake!

Ducks waddle past with their own sense of style,
One trips on a rock, but just grins with guile.
The sun sets in colors, a patchwork parade,
As day softly folds, its laughter won't fade.

Reflections abound in this tapestry bright,
Where joy finds a way, to shine in the night.
Nature's own canvas, a comical space,
In a world full of whimsy, we find our grace.

Radiance in the Breeze

Bumblebees dance in a floral spree,
Chasing petals, so wild and free.
Their giggles echo, a sweet delight,
As they buzz around with sheer delight.

Sunshine glimmers on each bloom's face,
A dandelion's fluff sways with grace.
The daisies whisper, a secret jest,
While the tulips strut in their Sunday best.

Butterflies join with a flamboyant flair,
Flitting about without a care.
They trip over nectar, wearing big grins,
As laughter blooms, the fun begins!

In this garden of joy, smiles take flight,
As petals waltz in the warming light.
The breeze carries tales of tomfoolery,
In nature's play, we find our jubilee.

Saffron Secrets

A quirky saffron with tricks to share,
Makes pasta do flips, it's quite the affair!
With giggling noodles and sauce so bright,
They twirl on the plate, a comical sight.

Curry concocts a mischievous grin,
As spices jump in, it's a flavor win!
Garlic joins dressed as a dancing fool,
While onions weep, breaking the rule.

Chili peppers wear capes, feeling bold,
In the spice rack, their stories unfold.
With laughter and rice, they all unite,
Creating a feast that's pure delight.

So let's savor this savory spree,
In saffron's charm, let's laugh with glee.
In every bite, a secret sparked,
Where flavors burst, and joy embarked.

A Tapestry of Sunbeams

With yarns of light, the sun weaves play,
In the fabric of day, let's frolic away.
Through giggling clouds, the sunlight dashes,
Knitting rainbows before it clashes.

Shadows chuckle beneath the trees,
As squirrels chatter and dance with ease.
The daisies tease in a sunbeam race,
While butterflies prance, putting on a face.

Knitted strands of golden hue,
Tickle the flowers, urging them too.
Each petal twirls in a gleeful scrimmage,
As nature creates its own sweet image.

So, grab a sunbeam, let laughter reign,
In this sunny tapestry, joy is our gain.
Together we stitch moments divine,
In the warmth of light, our spirits intertwine.

Luminous Gardens Awaken

Dew drops laugh on a sparkling morn,
As sleepy buds stretch, feeling reborn.
With sleepy faces, the flowers yawn,
While sun-kissed laughter spills on the lawn.

Bees in pajamas, so fluffy and cute,
Begin their day with a sweet buzzed pursuit.
The zinnias giggle at the sight so grand,
As pansies play hopscotch across the land.

The lilacs dance with an elegant spin,
While tulips blush with a cheeky grin.
The humor of nature, oh what a joke,
As petals frolic and leaves softly stoke.

In this garden where laughter prevails,
The joy of spring never fails.
A bright serenade where whimsy thrives,
In luminous gardens, the spirit derives.

Honeyed Reveries

In the garden, bees do dance,
Wearing stripes like a circus prance.
They sip from flowers, oh what a spree,
Mixing pollen with a hint of glee.

Buzzing tales of sweet delight,
With each bloom, they take a bite.
Nature's sugar, oh what a treat,
Making midday feel so sweet.

Beware the honey, sticky and thick,
Laughter bubbles, it's quite a trick.
Drip, drop, on toast it goes,
Sticky situations, as everyone knows.

In every jar, a giggle hides,
As I spread it wide, my sandwich slides.
But with that crunch and that sticky cheer,
Honeyed dreams are always near.

Serenade of the Scented Breeze

In the air, the scents collide,
Flowers giggle, petals wide.
With a breeze that sneezes fun,
Nature's song has just begun.

Daffodils and daisies wink,
Their floral fun makes you think.
Who knew a garden could be so loud,
With scents that giggle, oh I'm so proud!

Bees are buzzing, what a fuss,
Chasing scents on a vibrant bus.
They bump and tumble, what a sight,
In this frolic, all feels right.

Sunflowers stretch, they twist and bend,
Making each other laugh, my friend.
In this fragrant, joyous tease,
A serenade in the scented breeze.

Canvas of Nature's Palette

Splashes of color on nature's quilt,
Every petal with laughter is built.
Brush strokes of yellow, pink, and green,
A joy-filled canvas, oh what a scene!

With dandelions tossing their hair,
Painting the sky, a colorful flair.
"Who needs a painter?" they seem to say,
"Join us for fun in a floral display!"

Bumblebees wear their fashion bold,
Strutting their stripes like pieces of gold.
They dance on petals, a cheeky parade,
Creating a scene that never can fade.

Nature's joke in a splash and swirl,
A masterpiece that makes you twirl.
With laughter blooming, colors ignite,
A canvas of cheer, pure delight!

Celestial Hues of Growth

Sprouts have secrets, roots entwine,
They giggle softly, feeling divine.
In soil's embrace, they stretch and play,
Singing songs of growth every day.

With morning dew, their smiles shine,
They wink at clouds, "This sun is mine!"
Rays of light tickle each leaf,
Nature's laughter, what a relief!

Worms in the dirt share jokes so sly,
With each wiggle, a chuckle flies.
"I'm the underdog, what's my score?"
"Two bursts of soil, then wiggle some more!"

As flowers blossom, colors burst,
In every petal, there lies a thirst.
For laughter, joy, and a little cheer,
In celestial hues, we hold so dear!

Harvesting Light

In fields of fuzz, the bees all dance,
They look so silly, as they prance.
With tiny buzz, they take their flight,
Harvesting joy, from dawn till night.

Sunshine spills on petals bright,
A rainbow shimmer, quite a sight.
Bees wear shades, they're oh so cool,
In nectar pools, they splash and drool.

They giggle as they bump and crash,
In pursuit of pollen, they make a splash.
With every dive, they crack a grin,
Gathering sweetness, let the fun begin!

At dusk they buzz, their day complete,
With tales of clover and floral treat.
Back to the hive, they share their lore,
In the world of flowers, there's never a bore!

Blooming in Liquid Gold

In gardens lush, the flowers wink,
They know they're sweet, don't need to think.
A buzzing crew, they come around,
With silly hats, they're nectar-bound.

Dripping dew like liquid gold,
In this sticky mess, they won't be cold.
With tiny legs, they dance with flair,
Making us chuckle, without a care.

Pollen fights in the summer sun,
Who's the stickiest? It's all for fun!
They hoard their treasures, oh what a sight,
In this game of pollen, they pollinate bright.

At day's end, they giggle and boast,
About their wild, sweet-golden toast.
In every bloom, they find delight,
A party of flowers, it feels just right!

Enchanted by Sweetness

Oh, what a buzz in the flowery land,
With bees and blooms that go hand in hand.
They're sipping sweet from a petal's grin,
With laughter bubbling from deep within.

Daisy chains and lilac cheers,
Fill the air with delights and jeers.
A honeyed fate, it's all so funny,
They frolic about, like little honey buns!

Each flower whispers, 'Join the dance!'
And they're like kids, who take the chance.
With silly stunts and gentle hugs,
These buzzing bees are flower bugs!

As sunset glows, their work is done,
They tip their hats, 'Oh, what fun!'
In sweetness gathered, so much to share,
With honey laughter filling the air!

Threads of Sweet Solitude

In quiet corners, where flowers grow,
Bees weave their magic, a vibrant show.
With tiny feet, they thread in and out,
In the dance of blooms, there's never a doubt.

A dandelion's wishes take to the skies,
While bees in tuxedos, play tricks and lies.
They buzz with glee, "It's our secret game!"
In the thread of sweetness, they make their name.

With laughter that tumbles, like soft summer rain,
They tickle each petal, do it again!
In solitude's charm, they find their fun,
Creating a tapestry, just for the sun.

At twilight's giggle, they rest their wings,
Reflecting on all the joy that spring brings.
In solitude's threads, they've captured delight,
A secret dance, in the cool of the night!

Nature's Gilded Echo

In the meadow, bees do play,
Chasing flowers, what a day!
Daisies giggle, tulips sway,
As sunshine winks, it's time to stay.

Butterflies wear shoes so bright,
Dancing round with pure delight.
Hummingbirds in silly flight,
Making nectar, what a bite!

A frog jumps in, a splash of cheer,
Sings a tune that all can hear.
Nature's laughter, loud and clear,
Join the fun, come and appear!

Then a squirrel with acorn hat,
Hiccups loud, now how 'bout that?
Nature's party, come and chat,
A giggle here, a punny spat!

The Alchemy of Blossoms

In the garden, colors dance,
Every petal gets a chance.
Bumble bees in their romance,
Swirling round in silly prance.

Tulips bow with grace and flair,
Roses blushing, unaware.
Daffodils beyond compare,
Tickling noses, so beware!

A ladybug, with style and grace,
Shows off dots in a bug race.
Worms wear suits, a tux parade,
Laughing in their earthen shade.

Pollen grains, they float and zoom,
Creating chaos, sweet perfume.
Nature's work, a wacky room,
Where laughter springs, and joys bloom!

Wings of Melodic Savor

Up in the sky, birds write songs,
Sparrows giggle, sing along.
Feathers fluffy, oh so strong,
Cracking jokes, it won't be long.

A crow caws in a silly pitch,
While robins dance, they swish and twitch.
Nature's music, quite the niche,
Bringing laughter, scratch that itch!

Crickets chirp in perfect tune,
Mice in hats say, "Not too soon!"
Frogs join in, a green festoon,
All in good fun, beneath the moon.

So join the choir, don't delay,
Nature's stage, come out and play.
With every note, come what may,
Life's a song, hip-hip-hooray!

Manna from the Meadow

In the meadow, snacks abound,
Grasshoppers jump, with leaps profound.
Picnics scattered on the ground,
Where laughter echoes all around.

Ants in line, they march like troops,
Gathering crumbs for all the groups.
Bugs in shades, sipping from loops,
Nature's party, woozy whoops!

Beetles tap their tiny feet,
To the rhythm, oh so sweet.
While caterpillars munch and eat,
Savoring leaves, a tasty treat!

From daisies, snacks fall like rain,
Every bite, a hearty gain.
Join this feast, it's not in vain,
Mirth in nature, wild and plain!

Radiance in the Meadow

Butterflies wear hats made of leaves,
The flowers gossip, sharing their thieves.
A ladybug plays hopscotch so bright,
While grasshoppers chuckle, what a funny sight!

Bees buzz around like they're at a show,
Practicing dance moves, putting on a glow.
Daisies roll over, just can't contain,
Their laughter erupts like a soft summer rain.

The sun grins down, with a twinkle and wink,
While ants march in sync, not stopping to blink.
Each petal giggles, adorned in pure glee,
In this meadow of mirth, where all want to be!

So come join the fun, bring your own hat,
In a world where each creature is splendidly fat.
Let's dance in the hues, let our worries all flee,
In this meadow of joy, wild and free.

Echoes of Petal Pathways

Walking on petals, oh what a treat,
With wobbling daisies that dance on their feet.
A squirrel on a swing, giggling loud,
Chasing the sunbeams through the playful crowd.

The roses debate who smells the best,
While tulips perform in a colorful jest.
Butterflies act as the best judges, too,
With scores made of laughter in the blossoming hue.

There's a hedgehog in glasses, reading a book,
While crickets serve snacks from a tiny nook.
Each leaf is a ticket to a fun little ride,
On pathways of petals where nobody hides.

Hurry along now, don't miss the parade,
With giggles and wiggles in every shade.
These echoes of joy in the flowery space,
Leave you chuckling and smiling, just in case!

The Dance of Sunbeams

Sunbeams twirl, like ballerinas aglow,
Tickling the flowers where wild breezes blow.
A rabbit in slippers joins in the fun,
As laughter erupts, oh what a run!

Petunias and pansies put on a show,
With rhymes that cause giggles wherever they go.
The daisies throw confetti up high,
While butterflies glide, taking to the sky.

A caterpillar raps, oh what a beat,
As beetles spin records from under their seat.
The sun winks at everyone passing by,
In this whimsical dance where joy jumps high.

So come take a chance, let your worries escape,
Join the dance of sunbeams in this colorful shape.
In the garden of laughter, we're all just one,
Where the music is sweet and the fun never shuns.

Lullabies of the Blossoms

When the moon whispers, blossoms will hum,
With crickets composing a symphonic drum.
A bumblebee croons, swaying from side to side,
Working a rhythm, under stars open wide.

Night-blooming flowers boast of their dreams,
Of candy-colored thoughts and chocolate moonbeams.
A sleepy hedgehog rubs his tiny eyes,
While starlight tickles the night's sweet sighs.

Fireflies twinkle, dancing to the tune,
Casting playful shadows under the moon.
They giggle and flutter, swirling around,
In the lullabies sung by the blossoms found.

So lay on the grass, let your giggles rise,
Beneath the soft glow of starry skies.
In this night full of laughter, dreams take their flight,
With lullabies that echo till morning light.

Serendipity in Sunlight

In the morning light so bright,
A bee tripped over a delight.
He buzzed a tune, danced in the air,
With every flower, he showed no care.

A dandelion tossed in the breeze,
Made friends with ants, a sight to seize.
They giggled loud, as pollen flew,
This funny gang had much to do.

A sunbeam winked, said 'come and play,'
While squirrels chuckled in their own way.
Who knew a flower could cause such glee?
Nature's comedy is plain to see!

So, in the grass, they had a ball,
With petals soft, they answered the call.
A laughter shared under skies so blue,
Proof that joy in sunlight is never through!

Luminal Butterflies

A butterfly in polka dots,
Swirled around in quirky spots.
She laughed at a snail, oh so slow,
While twirling round the garden's glow.

With wings like candy, bright and loud,
She zipped past a big, fluffy cloud.
A bee in shades tried to keep pace,
But lost his way in a flowery space.

"Catch me if you can!" she mocked with glee,
As frogs croaked jokes 'neath the willow tree.
While worms in soil giggled below,
Tickled by roots dancing in a row.

So tweet the tune of this funny flight,
In nature's rhythm, the world feels right.
With laughter blooming everywhere,
Who knew such joy lived in the air?

The Elixir of Nature's Bounty

A squirrel brewed a nutty stew,
With mushrooms plucked in evening dew.
He stirred with flair, the pot did hop,
A smelly mess, but he wouldn't stop.

The rabbits sneezed from the whiff so bold,
While flowers giggled, their stories told.
"Is dinner ready?" asked a curious mouse,
"Or is it just a scent from the house?"

A crow cawed loud, "What's in the mix?"
"Just a pinch of trouble," said the pixie tricks.
They all chimed in, "Let's give it a shot!"
If it's horrible, at least it's hot.

From nectar sweet to roots so wild,
This elixir turned plain days beguiled.
Nature's laughter boiled with joy,
In every cup, a giggly ploy!

Celestial Harvest

Up in the sky, the stars did chat,
About the planets and a flying cat.
"Did you see how he jumped?" they chimed,
With twinkling eyes, they laughed in rhyme.

The moon threw a harvest ball, you see,
Planted silver seeds for all to be.
While comets danced with a cosmic flair,
Tickling each star with a glittering care.

But what a mess with floating cheese,
Every bite met a mild squeeze.
The sun cracked jokes, bright as could be,
While clouds rolled in with a giggly spree.

So gather 'round, in the cosmic way,
Every star has something to say.
As laughter blooms beyond the scope,
In this celestial harvest, we soar with hope!

the tapestry of fragrant sighs

In a garden where daisies wink,
The roses gossip, tip a drink.
Sunflowers dance in a silly jig,
While lilies giggle, oh so big.

Bees wear hats, oh what a sight,
Buzzing round, taking flight.
Butterflies throw a lavish ball,
In this floral realm, they have a ball.

Tulips tell jokes; oh what a tease,
While breezes carry laughter with ease.
Petals whisper secrets and sigh,
Underneath the watchful sky.

Violets giggle, tickled pink,
Collecting stories, don't you think?
In this garden where blooms conspire,
Every flower fuels the laughter fire.

simmering dreams in garden hearts

In pots of clay, dreams bubble high,
Plants plot mischief, oh my, oh my!
Herbs in aprons, stirring away,
Cooking up fun in a cheeky play.

Cucumbers giggle at the tomatoes,
While chives sing tunes, away it goes!
Radishes roll in a fit of glee,
Unruly roots, wild as can be.

Peppers pop with a spicy jest,
While carrots compete for the funniest quest.
With leafy wigs and a tangerine toast,
These garden friends are the ones I like most.

In this patch of laughter and light,
Where dreams simmer and hearts take flight,
Nothing's too silly, not a fuss,
In this garden, it's all about us!

threads of creation unfurling

Threads of green winding through the land,
Stitching together with a whimsical hand.
Spiders weave tales of humor and cheer,
As they spin their webs without any fear.

Worms wear spectacles, reading the soil,
Composting jokes while they toil.
Seedlings sprout with a comedic flair,
Barking out laughter they want to share.

The sun blinks down, it's part of the game,
While clouds roll by, puffing with fame.
Each thread of nature, it seems to grin,
In this tapestry where giggles begin.

Laughter blooms with every slight breeze,
Nature's humor dances with ease.
Creating a quilt of joy, we find,
A tapestry where love is entwined.

soaring between the blooms

High in the treetops, a squirrel swings,
Juggling acorns while the robin sings.
Daisies wave as they catch the show,
In this garden where giggles grow.

Butterflies flutter with sass and might,
Chasing each other, what a sight!
Between the blossoms, they play and dart,
A fluttering dance that warms the heart.

Ladybugs wear polka dots so bright,
Rolling down petals, what pure delight!
Every flower joins in the fun,
As nature's laughter is never done.

So here we soar, on joy's sweet breeze,
Between the blooms, with such ease.
In this garden, forever we'll stay,
Laughing our worries far away.

The Whispers of Sunlit Fields

In fields where bees do zoom and sway,
The flowers giggle, come what may.
They tickle bees with vibrant charms,
While sunlight basks in floral arms.

The daisies tease the dandelion,
"Oh look, you've lost your lion's mane!"
With laughter shared, so light, so bright,
They sparkle under golden light.

A bumblebee dressed in a suit,
Sips nectar from a flower's flute.
"Hey buddy, where's your fancy hat?"
"Oh, it's stuck! I sat on that!"

Amidst this joy, the breeze then twirls,
As petals tumble, dance, and swirl.
Nature's jesters, bright and spry,
In sunlit fields, the giggles fly.

Drifting in Botanical Bliss

A flower stretched, so proud, so tall,
Said to the breeze, "Come have a ball!"
Together they twirled with glee,
In that grand garden jubilee.

The roses winked at pansies near,
"Join us, come, we have no fear!"
With petals fluffed, they jumped and cheered,
While onlookers giggled, unappeared.

A butterfly, all dressed in style,
Sipped from blooms and flashed a smile.
"Why did you stop?" the violets cried,
"I was just practicing my glide!"

They spun around in happiness,
As daisies dropped their dress of stress.
In botanical hilarity, they find
A world of laughter intertwined.

Whispers of Sunlit Nectar

In gardens rich with vibrant hues,
The flowers whisper silly news.
"Did you hear the peony's song?
It's off-key, yet we sing along!"

Daffodils peek from daydreams wide,
"Who wore that silly hat?" they chide.
"It's just a bee with a grand disguise,
He's buzzing high but can't touch the skies!"

Sunflowers sway, a raucous crowd,
"Who stole my shade?" they laugh out loud.
As petals puff, they spin and stretch,
In sunshine's warmth, all woes they fetch.

Just then, a squirrel on the run,
Joined the dance, so quick and fun.
With all the blooms, a joyful play,
Sunlit nectar brightens the day.

Nectar's Dance in Twilight

As twilight whispers, blooms unite,
They share their tales, both sweet and bright.
The hummingbird hums jokes untold,
While petals blush in shades of gold.

A ladybug with polka-dots,
Sips nectar from the biggest pots.
She told the lilies, with a wink,
"Let's paint our petals, what do you think?"

The moonbeam watched from afar,
As they danced under a twinkling star.
"Are we not late for the ball?" they exclaimed,
With laughter echoing, none were blamed.

In twilight's glow, they twirled with glee,
Creating ripples of floral jubilee.
In nature's embrace, they took a chance,
And swayed in sync to nectar's dance.

www.ingramcontent.com/pod-product-compliance
Lightning Source LLC
Chambersburg PA
CBHW072145200426
43209CB00051B/459